BE STILL AND KNOW THAT I AM GOD

Patricia Gits Opatz

THE LITURGICAL PRESS
Collegeville, Minnesota

Nihil obstat: Joseph C. Kremer, S.T.L., *Censor deputatus.*

Imprimatur: ✚ George H. Speltz, D.D., Bishop of St. Cloud, Minnesota, April 13, 1981.

Cover design by Mary Jo Pauly.

| 3 | 4 | 5 | 6 | 7 | 8 | 9 |

Copyright © 1981 by The Order of St. Benedict, Inc., Collegeville, Minnesota. All rights reserved.

Printed in the United States of America.
ISBN 0-8146-1231-8

Contents

Introduction 5
Chapter 1 Be Still. 8
         2 Self-Fulfillment 17
         3 Patience. 29
         4 Rejoice Always? 40
         5 The Comforter 50
         6 Ordinary Holiness 60

Introduction

A friend once observed to me that the ideal wedding gift would be a set of three books: a dictionary, a cookbook and a Bible. I like the idea of the Bible being considered of as much practical value as a book full of recipes. This very thing is a discovery which increasing numbers of ordinary Christians are making every day: that Scripture has something vitally important to say to them about their real lives in the real world, that it is not merely a body of abstract knowledge to be left to the private concern of the scholars and experts, like Einstein's theory of relativity or the existence of black holes in space.

This should really come as no surprise. If we look at what Scripture itself says about the Word of God, we discover there is nothing at all remote or abstract about it. For example, the psalmist says that the Word of God is "a lamp to my feet . . . a light on my path" (Ps 119:105), surely a useful and reassuring aid. Jesus himself, calling upon Scripture for strength in time of temptation, compares it to bread: "Not on bread alone is man to live, but on every utterance that comes from the mouth of God" (Matthew 4:4). What could be more down to earth than bread? Calling the Word of God "living and effective," Paul too affirms that Scripture is meant to be a source of comfort and strength in our lives. The articles and questions in this booklet are firmly rooted in this belief—and in the hope that readers may find them helpful in experiencing the strength of the Word in their own lives.

This booklet might be useful for Bible study groups looking for a somewhat different way of studying Scripture—not going through one book chapter by chapter, but reading passages from many parts of Scripture relating to a particular theme from life. In this case, each member would be encouraged in advance to read the scheduled chapter pencil in hand, noting questions, comments or personal experiences brought to mind in the reading. These along with the article would begin the discussion. Next the questions and Scripture references would be read and responses shared.

Families too might find the booklet useful for study, and would have the advantage of participation by family members at different stages in life. Wouldn't it be interesting to get the reactions of a person of high school age and a seventy-year-old grandparent to the same subject — say, what it means to be patient, or fulfilled, or holy?

On the other hand, there may be some individuals who would prefer to read the booklet privately, using the questions for personal reflection and prayer.

Whether in a group or alone, may all who use this booklet experience the Word of God to be as nourishing as bread and as comforting as a light on their path.

1

Be Still

On the front page of the morning paper was a headline about the new noise control ordinance passed by the city council. Garbage trucks would not operate before six A.M., mufflers would be spot checked, trucks would be restricted to established routes, decibels of noise would be measured at specified trouble spots about the city. It was, according to the article, a model ordinance being examined by other cities across the country. To explain the need for such a new law, various studies were cited which showed how damaging to human beings excessive, incessant noise can be.

Sometimes it seems that we need such a noise pollution ordinance for our own inner lives as well as for our cities. Perhaps the model ordinance for us could be the one issued by God in Psalm 46: "Be still and know that I am God."

One of the key words in the sentence is "still," a word with several lovely meanings. For one thing it can mean silence; to be still is to be quiet, silent. It can also mean calm, as when Jesus calmed the stormy sea, telling it to be still (Mark 4:39). It can mean to be motionless, to stand still, to *wait*. And in one of these ways or in all of them at once this line from Psalm 46 can bring help to any person, especially the harried, rushed person.

For example, we may find ourselves worrying too much. It may be about the children; they are sick or in trouble or not doing well in school. Or they may be hurting from what someone has done to them and we can't help. It may be family problems or money problems, or even the big problems of the world—war, hunger, poverty. Then we remember God's words: "Be still and know that I am God." Quiet your mind and trust me. I have charge over all these things. I will make all things work for the best if you just believe in me and be still. What can *you* do anyway?

The words can also help us when we take on too much, accept too many commitments, say yes too many times, and then wonder how we will ever be able to hurry enough to get it all done. We make lists and schedule every hour of the day in the effort to fit it all in, and we try to remember when was the last time we did something *not* in a hurry. Then God's word gives us a little reminder: "Be *still* and know that I am God"; calm down—trust me—let me help you—stop stewing and fretting. And it helps. It also helps us begin to put things in order and say no to things that we really should say no to without feeling guilty.

This word can nudge us sometimes when we simply talk too much. We find ourselves at the breakfast table haranguing one of the children, "Now dear, if you would just drink your orange juice and not try to drink your orange juice *and* read the paper at the same time, then it would go faster and you would have time to get your bed made before you go to school. Honestly when the older ones were home, they always got their beds made in the morning, and you never do." And on and on and on! "Be still and know that I am God"—it comes to us. Leave the child alone. I would rather see a few smiling faces around here than get those beds made.

Sometimes this talking too much happens in the time we set aside to pray. We feel we have to tell God everything in this one hour, every need, every problem, every sick or troubled person we have promised to pray for—talk, talk, talk. And the Lord says, "Be still and know that I am God." I know all of this already. Of course I want you to bring everything to me; after all, it was I who told you to cast your cares upon me and I would support you (Ps 55:23). But does it all have to be at one time? Why don't you calm down and be quiet and try listening for a change? Trust me; maybe I have something to say that you need to hear.

There are times too when we become very discouraged, especially about ourselves. We have the same faults we have been trying to get rid of for years. All our new year's resolutions are broken by the end of the first week in January; our Lenten resolutions fall by the wayside, and we seem to be making no progress at all. Then we ponder the line from Psalm 46: "Be still and know that I am God." Just hold very still, be calm and quiet, wait. You should know by now that it is usually in these dry times, these unrewarding times, that you grow the most—if you will only accept them and thank me for them quietly. Hold still—you cannot feel it yet, or see it, but I am working in you. And remember my friend, I am God, not you. It is *I* who will get rid of those faults and make you holy.

This same thought can help us when we find ourselves complaining over all the little sufferings

12 *Be Still and Know That I Am God*

that come into our lives. At those times, "Be still and know that I am God" means: Listen my dear, these little crosses I am sending you are not just off the rack somewhere. They are not insignificant, run-of-the-mill crosses for just anybody. These are custom designed for you. Each day's little burdens are exactly what you need for that day to do the most for you. But if you won't be still and accept them quietly, taking advantage of them, it will be an awful waste. Now be still, and make the most of these gifts I am giving you.

But sometimes, bearing another person's suffering is harder than bearing our own; seeing someone we love suffering with a terrible illness, or hurting dreadfully in a bad marriage, or being done an awful injustice, is more painful than if we had to bear it ourselves. If we can be still, quietly praying and relying on God's faithfulness, much good can come of even these hard things.

The ways in which this word of the Lord can instruct us seem almost endless. When we are tempted to be mean or critical of someone else, it says to be still and leave the judging to God, since only he can really know what is in the heart of another person. When we lie awake at night planning every minute of a particularly busy day, making mental lists and rehearsing conversations, it says to be at peace and leave things to God. When we keep re-living a past failure, experiencing the regret over and over again, it tells us to let go of that memory and to look forward with hope.

To be still in this sense is not to be passive or indifferent: actually it requires great activity of the mind and heart. It is the stillness of total trust.

We are told that God's word is a "lamp to our feet, a light on our path" (Ps 119:105), and so it can be with this line from Psalm 46. No doubt only a word that comes from God could fit so many situations from sick children to balancing the budget to spiritual hunger to sleepless nights. Those eight one-syllable words contain a great truth which is expressed in many other ways in the Bible, perhaps none more moving than the one in Isaiah where God says:

> You are my servant, . . .
> I have chosen you, not rejected you.
> Do not be afraid, for I am with you;
> stop being anxious and watchful,
> for I am your God.
> For I, Yahweh, your God,
> I am holding you by the right hand;
> I tell you, "Do not be afraid;
> I will help you" (Is 41:8-10).

For Discussion

1. Reflect on these two lines from Psalm 139:
   > Even before a word is on my tongue,
   > Behold, O Lord, you know the whole of it.

   How might understanding this thought help us be more "still" when we pray?

2. Read the incident from the prophet Elijah's life in the nineteenth chapter of 1 Kings. What does this tell us about the need for stillness in our own lives in order to hear what God is saying?

3. There is frequently a tension in our lives between our need for our own quiet inner life

and our obligations to the many communities we belong to. How successful can we be in serving others if we do not nourish that inner life? Read the story of Mary and Martha in Luke 10:38-42. Also read Mark 1:35, one of the many instances when Jesus went off by himself to pray.

4. In Psalm 32:1 we read:

> I said, "I will watch my ways,
> so as not to sin with my tongue;
> I will set a curb on my mouth."

James also has something to say about keeping our tongue under guard (3:1-12). And there are numerous references in Proverbs to watching our tongue (for example: 10:19; 13:3; 17:27). Read these passages and then discuss the relationship between keeping still outwardly and achieving inner stillness.

5. After the incident of finding Jesus in the temple (Luke 2:41-52), we are told that Mary "treasured all these things in her heart." What "things" do you think she must have pondered? What can we learn from Mary?

16 *Be Still and Know That I Am God*

6. The older translations of this line from Psalm 46 said, "*Cease striving* and know that I am God." What different insights into its meaning does this version give the passage?

7. The story is told of the bishop who admitted to his spiritual advisor that he was far too busy to spend a whole hour every day in prayer. The spiritual advisor said, "Then make it *two* hours—and prime time!" The bishop did, and found that somehow all of his work did get done. Jesus asked, "Could you not watch one hour with me?" (Matthew 26:40) Discuss ways you have devised to find a quiet time and place for prayer and stillness each day.

2

Self-Fulfillment

The second cup of coffee was being poured when the conversation turned to the subject of self-fulfillment. One of the women had just turned fifty, and she admitted she was feeling very *un*fulfilled, frustrated a bit, not satisfied with her life as she looked back on it from this vantage point. Turning to one of her friends, she asked, "How do you manage to seem so fulfilled?"

It sounds simple enough, but it is not really an easy question to answer. Imagine what your answer would be if someone asked *you,* "How do you achieve self-fulfillment?" Are you fulfilled? Do you know someone who is? What is self-fulfillment anyway? It is a subject much discussed these days.

Among the many dictionary definitions for "fulfillment," the two which seem to apply best in this situation are that fulfillment means to "bring into actuality" or to "develop the full potentialities of something," in this case one's self. Further, such a fulfillment leaves one satisfied, feeling a kind of completeness. The expressions "finding oneself" and "finding one's identity" frequently enter this discussion too. In fact there are numerous books on the subject which stress this aspect: *Pulling Your Own Strings, Looking Out for Number One, How to be Your Own Best Friend.* The implication clearly is that if we wish to be satisfied, we have to discover who we are and what our potential is — and then develop that by putting ourselves first.

It might be useful to take this view of self-fulfillment, which is the world's view, and hold it alongside the view of Scripture to see how it measures up. For as God says through Isaiah, "My thoughts are not your thoughts, neither are your ways my ways, for as the heavens are above the earth, so are my ways above your ways, and my thoughts above your thoughts" (55:8-9).

Someone might argue, "Ah, but what about the story of the talents, the parable in which Jesus makes it clear that we *are* to develop our potentialities, our talents?" That's quite true. Someone else might point out that we are told not to hide our light under a bushel, but to let it shine for the world to see. True again. But if we read both of those passages to the end, we see that it clearly is not a matter of "looking out for number one." Rather, those servants who were praised for developing the talents had done so for the Master. Their reward was from him, and it was an end result of having first of all done well *for him.* Similarly, the passage about letting our light shine ends: ". . . your light must shine before men so they may see goodness in your acts and give praise to your heavenly father" (Matthew 5:14). Again the purpose is not to develop the talents, or let the light shine for one's own sake primarily, but to satisfy the Master, to glorify the Father. The person's reward is secondary.

And that seems to sum up the difference between the world's view of being self-fulfilled and God's view: the world says we should seek self-fulfillment, pursue it—work at it for our own sake. God says in his Word that if we forget ourselves and serve him, the contentment of self-fulfillment will come as a by-product, without our having to work at it. He says this in a number of interesting ways, and they all come down to this: if

20 *Be Still and Know That I Am God*

we want to be fulfilled, fully developed persons, we must make ourselves servants of one another.

Examine this idea of "looking out for number one." Jesus too has something to say about that. In the Gospel where James and John request to sit at the Lord's right and left hand when he comes into his glory, Jesus tells them, "Anyone among you who aspires to greatness must serve the rest; whoever wants to rank first among you must serve the needs of all" (Mark 10:43-44).

He teaches the same lesson again at the Last Supper when he washes the feet of his followers and says, "What I just did was to give you an example: as I have done, so you must do. No slave is greater than his master; no messenger outranks the one who sent him." Significantly, he ends by saying, "Once you know all these things, *blest will you be* if you put them into practice" (John 13:14-17). The contentment, the self-fulfillment, the *blessing* will follow when we have made ourselves servants to each other.

St. Paul says the same thing in another way. He speaks of receiving not talents, but gifts, which in a sense are talents on the spiritual level. He makes it clear over and over in 1 Corinthians that whatever gifts we have received, however lowly or exalted they may be, are not for our own fulfillment, but for the good of the body, the whole community. If all members of the community lay down their lives, their gifts and their talents for the good of all, then all are fulfilled. My gifts help in your fulfillment and yours help in mine.

The passage which may best express the scriptural view of self-fulfillment and self-identity is in Matthew 10:39 where Jesus says, "He who seeks only himself brings himself to ruin, whereas he who brings himself to nought for me discovers who he is." In other words, the person who concentrates on discovering and fulfilling himself or herself will never make it; the one who concentrates on serving others will gradually discover and fulfill himself or herself as well. It is just one more variation on that theme which runs through all of the New Testament, the great truth that sounds like a contradiction: there is no life without death; he who loses his life will find it; there is no Easter without Good Friday; unless the seed falls into the ground and dies it will bear no fruit.

Well, it sounds great, but can it possibly work? This question was put to a class of high school sophomores who were studying a unit on marriage and the family. In discussing servanthood, they were asked to try to imagine what family life would be like if each person had this attitude of putting himself or herself last and being a servant to the others. For their assignment that week, they were asked to try doing that very thing in their own homes — without explaining to anyone what they were doing. The next week when they were asked to report, only one student had even tried it. And what was the reaction? "They thought I was crazy!" she said. She added that it had been a good experience, and she could see what a revolution it would be in a family if everyone did it.

Various writers have expressed the scriptural idea of servanthood in different ways. Derek Prince in his *Faith to Live By* writes about the image frequently used in Scripture of purifying gold and silver. He uses the image to apply to having one's faith tested by fire, but it applies equally well to the idea of emptying ourselves and becoming servants:

> In purifying gold and silver, the refiner of Bible times suspended the metal in a melting pot, over the hottest fire that he could produce. . . . As the metal seethed in the pot, the "dross" — that is, the impurities — was forced to the surface and was skimmed off by the refiner. This process continued until all impurities had been removed and nothing but the pure refined metal was left.

SELF-FULFILLMENT 23

> It has been said that the refiner, bending over the metal in his pot, was not satisfied of its complete purity until he could see his own image accurately reflected in its surface.[1]

So it is with people who become servants; the impurities of their selfishness are refined away until they are pure gold, truly what God intended them to be, to the point that when God looks at them he sees only himself. And so do we.

In his book *The Art of Loving,* Erich Fromm makes a somewhat similar comment when he discusses loving. Today, he says, people work very hard at becoming lovable.[2] We are urgently advised to smell sweet, have shiny hair, stay slim, dress young, to polish our conversation and manners—in short do everything we can to make sure that people find us lovable—a kind of self-fulfillment. The burden of his book is that it would be better for us to put all of that effort into being loving, not lovable, people. For the person who concentrates on being loving will inevitably be more lovable as well. Most of us can confirm this from our own experience: it is hard not to love

---

1. Derek Prince, *Faith to Live By* (Fort Lauderdale, Florida: CGM Publishing, 1977) 123-124.
2. Erich Fromm, *The Art of Loving* (New York: Bantam Books, Inc., 1963) 1.

a loving person. Here again if we put the emphasis on others, not on ourselves, fulfillment will come as a by-product.

On a more homely level this idea was expressed at a recent business convention by a psychologist who was speaking about how people build each other up and tear each other down. He observed that each of us starts our day carrying our "bucket"—that is, our feelings about ourselves. All day long we meet people who either put something into our bucket (when they show appreciation for us or affirm us in some way), or who dip into our bucket (when they disapprove or reject us in some way). And we in turn either put something into the buckets of those we meet, or we dip into their buckets and empty them. Sometimes at the end of a bad day there is nothing left in our buckets, and there is no way in the world we can refill them ourselves. But here is the secret: when we begin to fill other people's buckets, building them up and affirming them, we discover that our own buckets are full again.

No best seller on the market can do as good a job of making us self-fulfilled as the Lord can do if we try it his way. Whether we think of it as gold that is refined, as servanthood, or as a full bucket, we can be sure that it is something achieved not by concentrating on it, but by looking elsewhere instead. Thank God for his wonderful plan — his way, everybody gets fulfilled.

For Discussion

1. Perhaps no person in the Gospels stands out so clearly as a unique, wholly fulfilled person as does John the Baptist. All four evangelists write about him. (See Matthew 3, 14:1-12; Mark 1:1-8, 6:14-29; Luke 3:1-20; John 1:6-9, 19-34.) In all these readings, can you find any evidence that John sought anything for himself? Discuss John as an example of the fulfilled person who is a servant to others. Note especially Jesus' own testimony about John in Luke 7:18-28.

2. Read Phil 2:5-7 where Paul tells us our attitude must be that of Christ. If I have the attitude of Christ described there, does it mean I

have to be a doormat? How do I decide where my priorities lie? To what things can I — and should I — say "no"?

3. We hear so much these days about how crucial it is for a person to have a good self image. Won't putting myself last and serving others give me a bad self image? Isn't it a way of putting myself down? (It might help to recall those times when you did something really selfless. Did you feel put down? Diminished? How *did* you feel?)

4. Does this idea of servanthood sound too idealistic? Is it really possible for people to live this way? Doesn't it go against human nature too much? Is it something we can do on our own? In Psalm 103 we are told that God "knows how we are formed; he remembers that we are dust." And in John 2:25 we read that Jesus "needed no one to give him testimony about human nature. He was well aware of what was in man's heart." Knowing us this well, would he ask the impossible?

5. What should be my motivation for serving others? My own fulfillment or something else? Read Matthew 10:39 and see if you can recall and share with the group times in your life when you "discovered who you were" by serving someone else.

6. At the Last Supper Jesus tells his disciples, "Now is the Son of Man glorified and God is glorified in him" (John 13:31). He says "now," and yet what he faces in the next few hours is not glory, but suffering and death. Discuss the meaning of these words, and Jesus as the perfect model of becoming fulfilled ("glorified") through laying down one's life for others.

7. Read Luke 1:46-55, Mary's *Magnificat*. Discuss this prayer — and Mary — as they relate to self-fulfillment through being a servant to others.

3

Patience

The young expectant mother had just finished her visit to the doctor, frustrated and depressed because the baby was now a week overdue. "Ah, well, when the apple is ripe, it will fall," the old doctor told her, just as he had told hundreds of mothers before her over the years. Then he grinned, patted her on the shoulder, and gave her one last piece of advice:

Patience is a virtue; practice it if you can.
Seldom found in woman: *never* found in man!

She had ample opportunity over the years that followed to reflect on patience, for like most of us, she discovered that much of life involves waiting, and waiting involves patience.

Thinking about patience turns out to be something like peeling an onion layer by layer, because there are so many kinds and levels of patience and it crops up everywhere. Perhaps a good place to begin is with the word itself. "Patient" comes from a Latin word which means "to suffer." In fact, the synonym for patience in the list of the fruit of the Spirit is "long suffering" (Gal 5:22). And we know that the sick person, the person in the hospital is called a "patient," the one who suffers. No doubt waiting always involves some degree of suffering, whether it is the waiting for some joyful event to occur, or for some sorrow or suffering to end. Perhaps we have so much trouble with time because we were really made for eternity.

Patience at first glance appears to be an ordinary, garden-variety kind of virtue, not in a class with such noble virtues as faith, hope, charity, or justice. As we peel away more of the onion, however, we may discover that we have underestimated it.

One kind of patience we all recognize is the patience that mothers of small children perennially pray for, that calm evenness and cheerfulness of temper which does not lose control or become irritable or crabby. It is equally necessary

PATIENCE 31

for anyone who cares for or deals with people who are unpleasant or quarrelsome. One group of young mothers was disheartened when an elderly grandmother told them they would probably be praying for patience all their lives, not just when their children were small. Like most of us they had prayed, "Lord, give me patience — right now."

A second kind of patience is expressed in that poster which has been popular recently: "Be patient — God isn't finished with me yet." This can be a very consoling thought; it is the kind of patience which makes it possible for us to accept people exactly as they are and where they are. If we have a spouse, a loved one, or a teen-ager who has rejected the family's values, or who is clearly going astray, we do not abandon or write him or her off. God is not finished with them yet. His time schedule is not always ours. So we pray, do what we can to help, and patiently wait for God to finish his work in them, knowing that "there is an appointed time for everything" (Eccl 3:1).

A part of the same idea is that we can also be patient with ourselves because, thank heaven, God is not finished with *us* yet either. There are times in our lives when praying comes easily, when our faith is a joy and a comfort to us, and we feel we are making real progress. Then praying becomes a chore, bad habits rear their ugly heads again, and we become discouraged. This is when we need to be still, and patiently wait for God to continue working in us according to his own timetable. Gradually we come to recognize that these times of pruning can be the most fruitful of our lives.

There is another kind of patience which bears sorrow or loss without bitterness or complaining. It is not the grit-your-teeth, clench-your-fists kind of grim resignation, but a faithful acceptance — even embracing — of the suffering, knowing that in God's own good time, "all things work together for good" (Rom 8:28).

As we experience difficulties in cultivating patience, we can begin to appreciate God's patience with us. We see this in the parable of the weeds and the grain where the farmer is asked by his laborers whether they should pull out the weeds which have sprung up with the crop. But he tells them not to, lest the grain be destroyed too; better to wait until the harvest, he says, and separate the weeds out then (Matthew 13:24-30). Likewise God the farmer is patient with us and our weeds, giving us plenty of time and opportunity to grow before the final weeding out. So patient is the Lord, Scripture tells us, that to him "one day is as a thousand years, and a thousand years are as a day" (2 Pet 3:8). The same passage continues with the very comforting thought that "the Lord does not delay in keeping his promises—though some consider it 'delay.' Rather he shows you generous patience, since he wants none to perish but all to come to repentance" (2 Pet 3:9).

Perhaps we can begin to understand something of the magnitude of patience when we observe it in some of the great people of the Bible. Think of Abraham and the years he had to wait for that long-promised son—and of Sarah who waited with him so long that she laughed when she was told she could still be a mother. Think of Joseph, whose brothers sold him into slavery, and of what he had to endure before it became clear what God's plan was for him. We can think of Moses and his hard years in the desert; at the end he could not enter the promised land, but only see it from a distance. Or consider Paul, who spent long periods in prison even though he was doing the Lord's own work. Instead of railing against such interruptions he kept right on working, making those periods as fruitful as the ones he spent traveling. We can think of Jesus himself who spent most of his life quietly getting ready for his three years among the people. Many holy people —in the Bible and out of it—have waited with patience and never lost faith, even though such patience seemed like foolishness to others.

It becomes clear what a crucial virtue patience is when we consider how little progress there would be in the other virtues or in the life of the spirit without it. One can easily give up a meal for a starving person, but fasting the forty days of Lent takes patience. One can perform a heroic feat once, but it takes patience to lead a whole life of quiet heroism. One can readily forgive an offense or insult once, but it takes patience to forgive repeatedly. So it is with all the virtues and gifts: without patience, there would be no growth at all.

Impatient people, in a sense, try to play God, because they want to have the timing of things their way. Patient persons, on the other hand, have learned to wait for God's timing of things and to trust it. Really patient people manage to strike a perfect balance. They have the holy impatience (the "hunger and thirst") which longs for God to accomplish his work in us, to make us into what he has wanted us to be from the beginning, and at the same time the perfect willingness to leave it all up to God.

As usual the psalms say it all; we see both attitudes there. In one place the psalmist pleads:

> How long, O Lord? Will you forget me forever?
> How long will you hide your face from me?
> How long must I bear pain in my soul,
> > and have sorrow in my heart all the day?
> > > (Ps 13:2-3)

In another place, he tells us to "rest in the Lord and wait patiently for him" (Ps 37:7). Finally he gives us this comforting testimony: "I waited patiently for the Lord and he heard me" (Ps 40:1).

Suggested Reading

For the story of Abraham, read Genesis, beginning at chapter 12.

For the story of Joseph, read Genesis, beginning at chapter 37.

For the story of Moses, read Exodus, beginning at chapter 2, and Numbers, beginning at chapter 17.

For Discussion

1. Paul tells us in his letter to the Romans (15:4) that "everything written before our time was written for our instruction, that we might derive hope from the lessons of patience and the words of encouragement in the Scriptures." Recall some of those "lessons of patience" from the Scriptures. In what way can we derive hope from them?

2. In Isaiah 30:15 we read: "By waiting and by calm you shall be saved, in quiet and in trust your strength lies." Can you share with the group any experiences you may have had in which you were, in a sense, saved by calm

waiting, in which your strength lay in patience?

3. Read Psalm 107. It recounts numerous ways in which God took his people from the midst of misery and trouble and set them on a safe path. For example:

> They went astray in the desert . . . he led them to an inhabited city.
> They dwelt in darkness and gloom, bondsmen in want and chains . . . he led them forth . . . and broke their bonds asunder.
> They were stricken . . . he sent forth his word to heal them.

The last line asks, "Who is wise enough to observe these things and to understand the favors of the Lord?" In other words, the wise person is able to look back over the events of his or her life and see the hand of the Lord in them. If you were to write down the critical events of your life, would you be able to discern the ways God was with you and brought you safely through? How might such an exercise help you to have more patience in future trials? Can you give a few examples?

38 *Be Still and Know That I Am God*

4. The older translations of Hebrews 12:1 read, "Let us run with patience the race." Does it sound like a contradiction to *run* and be patient at the same time? Think of your own situation—are there times when you have to be patient and "run" at the same time?

5. The old catechism used to list the corporal and spiritual works of mercy. Among the spiritual works were "to counsel the doubtful," "to instruct the ignorant," "to comfort the sorrowful," "to admonish the sinner," but also included was "to bear wrongs patiently." This is not a going out in service to others, as the other works are, but rather an *interior* thing. How can bearing wrongs patiently be a work of mercy?

6. Is there such a thing as being too patient?

7. Discuss Paul's statement in his letter to the Romans (5:3-4) that "we know that affliction

makes for endurance [patience] and endurance [patience] for tested virtue, and tested virtue for hope." Have you observed this to be true?

4

Rejoice Always?

The young man pulled off his stocking cap, stomped the snow from his boots and slipped through the door into the last pew in church. He was late. By the time he had picked up a missalette and collected his thoughts, he recognized the song the choir was singing: "Rejoice in the Lord always. Again I say rejoice!" He didn't know whether to laugh or cry. His wife and children were in bed with the flu, he had had to borrow his neighbor's jumper cables to get the car started, and just before he reached the end of the driveway the snowplow had gone through, leaving a three-foot bank for him to shovel out. He should rejoice? All he could do was think St. Paul had let himself get carried away when he wrote that one.

It does sound a little hard to believe. How can anyone rejoice always? Of course we find it easy to rejoice over the good things, the times when we are celebrating, or even when we are merely content. But when the hard times and difficulties come, we consider ourselves doing very well indeed if we can grit our teeth and offer them up without too much complaining. Still, Scripture is quite specific about it. Paul tells us to rejoice always and thank God for everything (1 Thess 5:16-18). For everything? The headache, the disappointments, the friend who lets us down, the troublesome neighbor, the car that won't start, the washer that breaks down? And what about the big things—sickness, pain, death? There is simply no getting away from it; Scripture tells us we are to rejoice always.

It seems clear that this kind of rejoicing is something special, a joy not necessarily connected with our feelings. It is the kind of rejoicing that can be done even in the midst of fear and suffering, when we do not feel any of the delight or joy normally associated with rejoicing. In fact the dictionary definitions are not really adequate to encompass this scriptural kind of rejoicing. Several dictionaries say that to rejoice means "to feel great joy" or "to have feelings of great joy." If that is true, then how can we rejoice even when we do not have those feelings? No, this is something deeper.

Although this mysterious idea of always rejoicing goes against the grain at the natural level, it is deeply embedded in Scripture, in the Old Testament as well as the New. In Psalm 2, for example, we see rejoicing coupled with fear and trembling, certainly an unexpected combination:

> Serve the Lord with fear, and rejoice before him; with trembling pay homage to him (Ps 2:11-12).

Psalm 22 is a longer example of a similar thought. For most of the first twenty-two verses the speaker is describing his agony in vivid detail. It is the psalm Jesus prayed on the cross: "My God, My God, why have you forsaken me?" We are familiar from the Good Friday liturgy with the suffering depicted so graphically. Yet as the psalm continues, the suffering speaker turns to praising and rejoicing over the goodness of God. He tells the lowly, and he evidently includes himself among them, that their hearts should be merry (v. 27).

Another dramatic example of rejoicing in the midst of sorrow appears in the book of the prophet Habbakuk:

> For though the fig tree blossom not
> > nor fruit be on the vines,
> Though the yield of the olive fail
> > and the terraces produce no nourishment,
> Though the flocks disappear from the fold
> > and there be no herd in the stalls,
> Yet will I rejoice in the Lord
> > and exult in my saving God (Hab 3:17-19).

This sentiment would be akin to a modern speaker rejoicing when his home is gone, his business has failed, he is bankrupt, and he has few if any prospects for the future. How many of us would find rejoicing our first response in such a situation?

Although St. Paul is the major spokesman in the New Testament for rejoicing always, the idea is expressed in other places. Consider the scene after the resurrection when the women seek the body of Jesus and find the tomb empty. After confronting the angel, we are told, they hurry away "in fear and great joy," again an unexpected combination. Another translation says they are "half fearful, half over-joyed" (Matthew 28:8).

We find it also in the beatitudes where we read Jesus' words:

> Blest [happy] are you when they insult you and
> > persecute you and utter every kind
> > of slander against you because of me.

Be glad and rejoice, for your reward
   is great in heaven (Matthew 5:11-12).

We see the idea again in Acts; after Peter and the other apostles had been whipped and imprisoned, they "for their part left the Sanhedrin full of joy that they had been judged worthy of ill-treatment for the sake of the Name" (5:41).

Paul echoes this from his own experience when he writes to the Colossians, "Even now I find my joy in the suffering I endure for you" (1:24). And he prays that they in turn may be "endowed with the strength to stand fast, even to endure joyfully whatever may come" (1:11).

In fact rejoicing in times of trouble is assumed to be an inescapable part of the life of God's ministers. In his second letter to the Corinthians Paul lists in striking detail what it is like to be a witness and minister for the Lord, and right along with all the other seeming contradictions in such a life, he says they "are sorrowful, yet always rejoicing" (2 Cor 6:10).

It is hard to escape the fact that Paul is speaking to Christians of all times — and so to us — when he writes, "Rejoice in the Lord always! I say it again. Rejoice! (Phil 4:4), and "Rejoice always, never cease praying, render constant thanks" (1 Thess 5:16-18). But how can we learn to do such an "unnatural" thing? Perhaps one help would be to learn to separate our feelings from our will—that is, to make a deliberate decision to rejoice when we do not feel like it. We could begin with small things, rejoicing and thanking the Lord for the little crosses and trials that come our way daily: the delays, the disappointments, the ache or pain, the teacher or student who is difficult, the co-worker who sets our teeth on edge, whatever it might be. We could pray, "Lord, I do not understand this difficulty, this set-back, this frustration — it's hard. But I choose to rejoice in it and thank you for it, because I know you will bring good out of it for me and turn it into a blessing." We can point out to God as we pray that he should please not look at our feelings — "The real me is over here in my will, and I *choose* to rejoice in this and all the circumstances of my life even though I do not feel like it." Gradually we will find that we can move on to accept with this interior rejoicing the more difficult trials that come our way.

There is something about rejoicing and thanking God for whatever happens that makes it easier for God to do things for us. It is a kind of letting go which gets ourselves out of the way and opens the door for God's power to go to work in our lives in often surprising ways. Such rejoicing and thanksgiving in all situations may be one of the hardest and riskiest parts of the Christian life we are leading, but it is probably one of the richest and most rewarding.

For Discussion

1. Discuss the relationship between faith and rejoicing—what part does trusting God have to play in being able to rejoice in times of trouble? What part does patience play?

2. We read in Nehemiah 8:10 that "rejoicing in the Lord must be your strength." In what way do you think rejoicing in the Lord could be a person's strength?

3. In Paul's words to the Thessalonians, we read that not only should we rejoice always and give thanks for everything, but also that we should "never cease praying" (1 Thess 5:16-18). How important a role do you think a

48 *Be Still and Know That I Am God*

prayerful life plays in being able to rejoice always?

4. Psalm 37 says, "Take delight in the Lord and he will grant you your heart's requests" (v. 4). Reflect on what it might mean to "take delight" in the Lord.

5. Madeleine L'Engele in her book *The Irrational Season* writes about the "Noes of God."[1] She says that God will sometimes say "No" to us only to lead up to a greater "Yes" later. We must learn, she says, to be calm when God says "No," confidently expecting a "Yes" to come. Looking back at your own life, can you discover times when God said "No," only to provide you with a beautiful "Yes" later? How could realizing this help you to rejoice always in the future?

6. We often hear people say, "Well, things always seem to work out for the best." Is there

---

1. Madeleine L'Engele, *The Irrational Season* (New York: Seabury Press, 1977) 87–98.

REJOICE ALWAYS 49

any difference between this and the act of trust needed to rejoice in troublesome times, in the scriptural sense?

7. Read the passage in Matthew where he describes the women at the tomb. (28:1-8) Put yourself in their place and try to imagine what thoughts were in their minds to provoke the fear and joy they felt.

5

The Comforter

More than thirty years ago a teacher observed to her students that we had experienced the Age of the Father in the Old Testament, the Age of the Son with the coming of Jesus, and now we were about to enter the Age of the Holy Spirit. Her students could not have said what she based that prophetic statement on, but many of them would no doubt agree now that we are beginning to witness that age. In those years the Holy Spirit was frequently called the forgotten member of the Trinity. There were few sermons about the Spirit, and those we heard were usually abstract and theological, certainly not personal. Now, however, we are becoming much more aware of the Spirit as a Person, not an abstraction, confirmation programs are being revitalized to have real impact on their students, and more and more Christians are conscious of the Spirit's work in their own lives.

There are many names given to this Gift Jesus said he would send after he returned to the Father (John 14:26), each one revealing a slightly different aspect of the Spirit's work in our lives. The Spirit is called the Paraclete, the Advocate, the Helper, and the Comforter—perhaps the most consoling title of all. The word "comfort" comes from the same root as "fortitude," which means "strength." As the Comforter the Holy Spirit is one who brings strengthening aid in time of trouble.

Jesus must have expected us to experience this Comforter in a very real way, for in Scripture he often tells his followers not to worry. "Fear nothing" (Luke 12:7). "Stop worrying" (Matthew 6:31). "Why be anxious?" (Luke 12:26). "Do not let your hearts be troubled" (John 14:1). "Do not live in fear, little flock" (Luke 12:32). Numerous times and in a variety of ways, Jesus assures his followers they have no reason to be anxious or fearful. When he returned to the Father he sent his Spirit to make this possible. The Spirit would give us the power to overcome worry, to be at peace, to be comforted.

52 *Be Still and Know That I Am God*

On the day after Pentecost, Peter tells the crowds at Jerusalem, "This Jesus . . . . exalted at God's right hand . . . first received the promised Holy Spirit from the Father, then poured this Spirit out on us" (Acts 2:33). He adds that this Spirit is poured out not just on them, but on their children and on "all those still far off whom the Lord calls" (Acts 2:39). And that's us. We are told the Spirit is poured out. It sounds so lavish and extravagant — not just doled out, a little portion for each one of us, but *poured* out. It is reminiscent of the lovely line from Luke where Jesus describes how generously the Lord will repay those who are themselves generous: "good measure pressed down, shaken together, running over" (Luke 6:38). This is the way the Lord gives his Spirit.

We are living in the Age of the Holy Spirit, bearing within ourselves this powerful, gentle Comforter. We should be the most joyful, worry-free people in the world. Yet this same age has been called by poet W. H. Auden "The Age of Anxiety." Every day we read about the quantities of tranquilizers being sold and consumed, about the numbers of people turning to drugs or alcohol to escape the stress of life, about suicides increasing even among the very young and the very old. We see more and more books giving advice on handling anxiety, self-help books to comfort and console people and to help them deal with life. Who would ever guess we have a powerful Comforter to do these things for us?

Perhaps the promises of Jesus about the Comforter seem just too good to be true. How could an all-powerful, infinite God really care deeply about our concerns—not just the big, earth-shaking crises, but even our small daily problems? Yet this is exactly what Scripture asks us to believe; we are assured we can safely "cast all our cares on the Lord" (Ps 55:23), and have complete confidence in him, for he is indeed a God "who bears our burdens" (Ps 68:20). Do we find it hard to accept this in the practical affairs of our own lives? Are we among the unbelievers who find such promises too good to be true?

Catherine Marshall, in her book *The Helper,* has some revealing things to say about this unbelief which keeps us from having complete confidence in the Comforter.[1] When most of us think of sin, she writes, we tend to think of those lists we make of our faults and failings, our individual acts of sinfulness. When Jesus speaks of sin, he

---

1. Catherine Marshall, *The Helper* (Chosen Books Publishing Co., Ltd., 1978) 101-105.

54 *Be Still and Know That I Am God*

speaks of unbelief. She refers to John 16:7-9, where Jesus says, "If I go, I will send the Helper to you. And when he comes, he will convince the world of sin . . . because they do not believe in me." Too often we do not think of unbelief as a sin, but are more likely to see it as a kind of "disability we really can't help."[2] We admire the faith of others, wish we had that same fervor, and perhaps feel a little sorry for ourselves that we do not. But rarely do we think of accusing ourselves of this sin and confessing it. Catherine Marshall faced this problem in her own life, and after much prayer and reflection came to a conclusion useful for all of us. She says, "Then the Spirit showed me that every time I reject Jesus' ability to handle any problem or problem area in my life, I am rejecting him."[3]

If we do not experience the Comforter in our times of anxiety and stress, perhaps what we need to do is recognize unbelief for the sin it is, confess it, and ask for a spirit of real repentance. We can make our own words of the man who asked Jesus to heal his son: "I do believe. Help my unbelief" (Mark 9:24).

2. Ibid. 102.
3. Ibid. 103.

A further help in learning to trust the Comforter might be found by turning to the psalms, particularly the lamentation psalms. (For example: Pss. 31; 56; 74; 116; 142) In his book *Praise: A Way of Life,* Fr. Paul Hinnebusch has an interesting chapter called "Praising God by Complaining," in which he shows how to use the lamentation psalms as our own.[4] In these psalms the speaker is really complaining to God, listing vividly all his troubles and griefs. He asks God to save him from these troubles, then expresses a firm confidence in God's mercy, and last of all turns to praise. The author makes it clear the psalmist does not blame God for the troubles, but does list them forcefully so there is no mistaking they are real. He also notes that in the psalms "trust" and "praise" are often used interchangeably, so when we praise God we trust him, and when we trust him we praise him.

Reading these psalms prayerfully we may gradually develop the same frame of mind the psalmist has: entrusting our cares to God, praising him, and confidently expecting his comfort and aid. In order to make these psalms more personal and meaningful, we might even substitute our own

---

4. Paul Hinnebusch, "Praising God by Complaining," *Praise: A Way of Life* (Ann Arbor, Mich.: Word of Life, 1976) 83-92.

list of "complaints" in the appropriate parts. Listing whatever is disturbing us—worry about the children, our job, a troubled marriage, sickness, finances—we lay it all before the Lord in vivid detail just as the psalmist does. Then from the heart we pray the lines entrusting these cares to the Lord. Last of all, in the psalmist's words, we praise God for always being faithful to his promises. Surely the Comforter will not resist such a prayer, but will console and strengthen us. After all, it was the Holy Spirit who inspired those psalms.

If we find ourselves being anxious and worried often, or if we simply want to deepen our confidence in God, these are two things we might do. First, we repent of whatever unbelief we may be guilty of and pray for greater trust in Jesus. Second, we make God's prayers our own, using the psalms to express our need, our trust, our praise. Eventually we will grow in confidence that the Father will continue to pour out his Spirit, "in good measure pressed down, shaken together and running over."

For Discussion

1. In the story of Mary and Martha (Luke 10:38-42), we read that Jesus chides Martha for being "anxious and upset about many things," while Mary rests quiet and confident at Jesus' feet. Discuss this scene as it relates to belief and unbelief. Are we more like Mary or Martha? (It is comforting to reflect that Jesus loved them both.)

2. When Jesus tells his followers not to worry or be troubled, he is not asking us to fool ourselves, to pretend there is no suffering in this life. On the contrary, he is very specific about suffering being part of the Christian life

(Mark: 8:34-38). So on the one hand he tells us to expect suffering and on the other not to be troubled. How can we do both?

3. The Holy Spirit can work in very dramatic fashion when he chooses, as in the rushing wind, tongues of fire, a whole house shaking (Acts 2:2-3). But most of the time we experience his comfort in such quiet ways there is a danger we might not even be aware of them as his work. Discuss ways in which this has happened in your life; for example, "happening" to read or hear the words that answered a particular need, meeting the right new person at a crucial time, finding the correct words to say when you thought you would be speechless, easing through a difficult situation you had dreaded. How might we become better at observing the small, loving ways the Comforter works?

4. Read Mark 16:9-14, and discuss the "disbelief and stubbornness" of the disciples.

5. Paul's letter to the Romans (8:26-27) makes it clear that one of the ways the Spirit comforts

us is in helping us to pray. Are you praying differently from the way you prayed ten years ago? Are you praying better? How did this come about? Can you recognize the work of the Comforter in it?

6. Read Matthew 6:19-34, part of the Sermon on the Mount. Find and discuss the things Jesus tells us specifically we must not worry about.

7. To experience the psalmist's attitude of complaint, trust, and praise, divide your group into two parts and read Psalm 22 aloud, alternating verses. Discuss your reactions to the psalm.

8. Read Psalm 56. Using it as a model, compose your own psalm, substituting your needs for the complaints of the psalmist. You can do this individually or as a group, stating personal needs or larger community needs.

6

Ordinary Holiness

When we were children we listened in awe to the stories of the great saints and martyrs: Peter crucified head down, Lawrence roasted on a gridiron, Sebastian pierced with arrows, Francis wedded to poverty. Today we hear and see accounts of not very different modern-day saints: Mother Teresa of Calcutta spending her life for the poor and sick of India, Fr. Maximilian Kolbe exchanging places with a condemned prisoner and being starved to death in a Nazi bunker, Archbishop Oscar Romero being shot to death as he offered Mass in his San Salvador cathedral. The lives of such holy men and women are held up to inspire and encourage us, but at times they can tend to discourage us instead. We know that we are all called to be saints, but the ordinariness of our lives hardly seems the stuff of which saints are made. We do not seem to belong to the same race as these great souls. Maybe we need to remind ourselves that God made far more small, ordinary souls than he made saints on the grand scale, so there must be something in even the quietest, most unimpressive life that God can use to make a saint if he wants to—and he does want to.

Those great souls who give their lives to God in heroic fashion may be likened to the man in the Gospel story who sold all he possessed to purchase the pearl of great price (Matthew 13:45-46), or the man who spent his entire fortune to buy a field where a treasure lay hidden (Matthew 13:44). Some of us, however, might find it easier to identify with Jacob, a hero from an Old Testament story (Gen 29:15-30). There was no quick purchase for him; he had to labor for seven years before he could marry the beautiful Rachel. Even after the seven years he was duped, given her sister instead. Before he could marry Rachel, he had to agree to seven more years of labor for his father-in-law. The whole story is told in only a few verses in the Bible. When we envision those fourteen years stretched out one day at a time, however, we begin to see how many individual acts of service

Jacob must have had to perform over that long period to earn *his* pearl of great price.

We might remember Jacob when we read Jesus' statement, "There is no greater love than this: to lay down one's life for one's friends" (John 15:13). Reading this, we may feel secure that there is little likelihood we will be called upon to lay down our lives for our friends or for our faith as the great saints did. But we feel this security only if we think of laying down our lives as a one-time, blood-letting thing. Actually, most of us *are* called upon to lay down our lives, but we are called upon to do it like Jacob, in bits and pieces every day for years, not all at once. And who is to say which is harder?

We lay down our lives any time we hand over a part of ourselves in the service of someone else. We lay down our lives in the simple performance of the duties of our vocation; or when we give our money, our time, our energies, our talents, our efforts, our undivided attention, in the service of others; or when we work until we grow weary doing what we are obligated to do or what we are given the special grace to do. There are many apparently ordinary people all around us who in such ways are laying down their lives for friends, family members, communities. Many of these are truly heroic, however inconspicuous they may be.

That we are called to holiness by doing ordinary things is clear from reading some of Paul's letters to the communities he established. Right along with his most profound teachings, he includes salty, practical advice on what kind of day-to-day lives these new Christians should be living. For example, he says these "saints" should be generous, "not sadly, not grudgingly, for God loves a cheerful giver" (2 Cor 9:7). In some letters Paul praises the generosity already shown by the people (2 Cor 8:1-5). In other places he emphasizes the importance of good family life (Eph 6:1-4), obedience to authority (Rom 13:1-4), kindness and fairness in speech: "Never let evil talk pass your lips; say only the good things men need to hear, things that will really help them" (Eph 4:29). These early Christians are also encouraged to be faithful in prayer (Eph 6:18), to pray for one another and for their leaders (1 Tim 2:1-2). Such bits of advice are found throughout Paul's letters, all of them plain ordinary things. This is not to say that they are *easy,* as anyone knows who has tried them, but only that they are easily available to all of us.

If we need inspiration and suggestions on how to lead a holy life in such small ways, we

64 *Be Still and Know That I Am God*

might look to someone who was an expert, St. Therese of Lisieux, who called her way to holiness the "Little Way." It was her way to do even the smallest, most insignificant acts as perfectly and lovingly as possible. She carried obedience to the point of leaving her writing in mid-word when the bell rang for prayers. She observed St. Paul's advice to "bear with one another lovingly" (Eph 4:2) so perfectly that one crabby old nun who was shunned by the other sisters came to her one day, and asked what it was about her that made Therese seek her out so often. Insults, menial tasks, annoyances, disappointments—Therese embraced them all with absolute patience—and without drawing any attention to herself. She appeared to be no different from any of her sisters in the convent. In fact, the story is told that when she lay on her deathbed Therese overheard two sisters talking about her, wondering what in the world poor Mother Superior would find to say about her in her obituary, since she had not really done anything! Yet just twenty-eight years after her death Therese was canonized, and in later years was made patron of France along with Joan of Arc, and co-patron of the foreign missions along with

St. Francis Xavier. She had lived only twenty-four years.[1]

Therese was like the person in Psalm 131, a good prayer for us who live plain, ordinary lives:

> O Lord, my heart is not proud,
> nor are my eyes haughty;
> I busy not myself with great things,
> nor with things too sublime for me.
> Nay rather, I have stilled and quieted
> my soul like a weaned child.
> Like a weaned child on its mother's lap.
> so is my soul within me.
> O Israel, hope in the Lord,
> both now and forever.

The image of the weaned child on its mother's lap is a vivid one, for weaning applies not just to a child weaned from the breast, but to our becoming detached from whatever formerly held us. The simple soul has been weaned away from ambition to experience extraordinary things, and is satisfied with a quiet inconspicuous life if that is what God wants for it.

Rather than envy those who are called to heroic deeds, we can be grateful that God has provided us with an ordinary way to holiness. We look more appreciatively at the places where we

---

1. Theodore Maynard, *Saints for Our Time* (Garden City, N.Y., Image Books, 1955) 288-304.

live and work, at the people we see every day, because we recognize in them our "little way." These are our daily opportunities to practice hospitality, generosity, patience, obedience, prayer — and all those other virtues which Paul recommended to our Christian ancestors, the first saints.

For Discussion

1. In Matthew 11:11 we read what Jesus says about John the Baptist. In what ways are we, "born into the kingdom of God," greater than John?

2. Read the letter to the Hebrews (13:1-19) where the author lays down some rules for them. Discuss these rules as they relate to your lives today.

3. Read Psalm 131 aloud together. Discuss what it says and whether you think it has any meaning for your lives.

4. Make a list of the people Jesus associated with, loved, admired. What kind of people were they? What kind of lives did they lead?

5. In Matthew 11:25 Jesus prays: "Father, Lord of heaven and earth, I offer you praise; for what you have hidden from the learned and the clever, you have revealed to the merest children." Discuss what this prayer means. You might consider also Matthew 18:3-4 as part of your discussion.

6. Read Matthew 25:31-46. Think about Jesus' words, "I assure you, as often as you did it for one of my least brothers, you did it for me." Discuss this as it relates to the importance of small things in making our lives holy. Jesus equates himself with his "least brothers." Aren't we also his least brothers and sisters? Doesn't this make our lives very important?

7. Poet Hilaire Belloc once wrote:
> Of courtesy—it is much less
> Than courage of heart or holiness;

> Yet in my walks it seems to me
> That the grace of God is in courtesy.

In what sense do you think the grace of God is in courtesy? Can you see courtesy as one of the ordinary means of holiness?

8. Think of people you know whom you consider to be holy. Analyze some of the things they do that make you think of them as saintly.

Notes